COUNTRY OF THE MINOTAUR

BREWSTER GHISELIN

UNIVERSITY OF UTAH PRESS

IV

COPYRIGHT © 1947, 1949, 1950, 1951, 1952, 1956,
1957, 1959, 1961, 1962, 1965, 1966, 1967, 1968, 1969,
1970 BY BREWSTER GHISELIN. ALL RIGHTS RESERVED.
LIBRARY OF CONGRESS CATALOG CARD NUMBER: 75-116761

THIS BOOK DESIGNED BY KEITH EDDINGTON

TITLE ILLUSTRATION BY V. DOUGLAS SNOW

FIRST EDITION

All the poems in this book have been published, "Sea" in The John Peale Bishop Memorial volume *A Southern Vanguard* and the others in the following periodicals: *Concerning Poetry, Encounter, The Georgia Review, The Hollins Critic, The Hudson Review, The Kenyon Review, Letteratura* (Florence), *Mill Mountain Review, New World Writing, Poetry, Quarterly Review of Literature, The Sewanee Review, The Western Humanities Review, The Western Review.*

BY BREWSTER GHISELIN:

Poetry
COUNTRY OF THE MINOTAUR — 1970
THE NETS — 1955
AGAINST THE CIRCLE — 1946

*Edited,
with an Introduction*
THE CREATIVE PROCESS: A SYMPOSIUM — 1952
        (Mentor Book paperback, 1955)

v

TO OLIVE

CONTENTS

VII

I   THE COUNTRY OF THE MINOTAUR — 3
BLACK VULTURES OVER GUAYMAS — 7
PURSUITS OF A CHIMERA — 9

II   THE CATCH — 15
THE NET BREAKER — 19
ORCA — 21
KILLER WHALE, INSHORE — 23
CARACARA — 25
PAX VOBISCUM — 25
MARLIN — 27
FOR THE *BESTIARY* — 31

III   SEA — 35
THE WHEEL — 51
APHRODITE OF THE RETURN — 59

IV   PROGRESS REPORT — 63
ON A MONUMENT: ORANGE EMPIRE TROLLEY MUSEUM — 65
CORTE MADERA HILL — 67
UPLAND — 71
SUM OF SUMMER — 71
AUGURY — 73

VIII

TRACT — 75
HIS BABYLONIAN HEART — 75
NOCTURNE: LAGUNA BEACH — 77
LIGHT — 79
VANTAGE — 81

V

IN SEARCH OF MAN — 85
LEARNING THE LANGUAGE — 89
ANSWERING A LETTER FROM A YOUNGER POET — 91
ASCENT — 95
TEACHING MY SONS TO DIVE FOR ABALONE — 97
MOMENT BY MOMENT — 99
LOVE LETTER — 101
RETURN TO THE NIGHT — 103
FOR LOVE: A SHIFT — 105

VI

OMAGGIO — 108
PORTO — 108
PRESENTE — 110
AUSTRO — 110
ANNUNZIAZIONE — 112
UOMO — 114

IX

"In mezzo mar siede un paese guasto,"
diss' elli allora, "che s'appella Creta,
sotto 'l cui rege fu già 'l mondo casto."

INFERNO, XIV

I

THE COUNTRY OF THE MINOTAUR

3

I Minos had round eyes and a shaggy bull-brown
Beard of curls the color of his face,
A blunt hand, bloody weapon of our race,
    A mind as dark as any now
With fear, like ours, of darkness in the mind.

Pasiphaë was pale. Poseidon's bull
Waiting for death, white as the island foam,
Lived on. Though fragile as a honeycomb,
    The queen conceived. How should it be
Of a king's sweetness? A horned child was born.

Doubt upon doubt doubled and darkened then
Over the cradle where a rumor slept.
The hushed palace hummed with a secret kept,
    Forgot the lineage of their king,
Minos, of bull Zeus and Europa born.

4

II Alone in a high valley of flowers leaning
To a turquoise triangle of sea,
I think of Minos and Pasiphaë
    Who gave the Minotaur to shame
And made their palace dreadful to explore.

No rough ruin is here, or sad olive
Rooting memory in stone, or fumitory
Blowing, as out of ash of the old story.
    Only because a man is here
This is the country of the Minotaur.

BLACK VULTURES OVER GUAYMAS

HARBOR: The hissing whistle of their wings dividing the light
          Above the red islands often lifted my head;
          And the sky, filled with the purpose of a hundred
                  hurrying vultures,
          Interpreted the sea, rustling its different sibilants.

TOWN: I felt a spell of blue sharpen the thorns of the earth;
          I heard the active town coursing its labyrinth
          Of bisque about the harbor and backward amid the hills
          Lie still, a mast of shell abandoned to the sun.

CEMETERY: And, past the last sharp shack and barefoot paths, I saw
          Walled-in dead monuments bedizened with awful love,
          Paper blossoms of fear and trivia of doubt.
          Then in my empty hand I read the palm of dust.

DESERT: Over all frozen eyes, the black doves of that waste
          Passed to its ashen edge where their consuming peace
          Became those distances, westward the ocean plain,
          Landward a sea of light, the opal stare of haze —

GARDEN: Calcine of rose, old ash, quick with Arabian flame:
          A line of egrets wavering eastward over the waves,
          A whitewinged dove in the dove-loud green of a carob bough
          Over the fearless dead and the shade of the blowing tree.

PURSUITS OF A CHIMERA
(HOMOCANIS CONCOLOR)

I   Hounds are scraping the dark with hoarse nightbarking,
    Clawing our sleep as if they scented crime —
    Odor of act or of dream — or beautiful thing,
    Innocence, still as dogwood's floating hour
    Where the wood ends windless, before the axe.

    The evil hear that dissonance rouse and come.
    And the most living, who explore the light
    Far from our ways, hear — for a pathless place
    Will draw the hounds' assault — and feel their hands
    Yield up like blood the immeasurable sun.

    If you are lost, the unperplexed police
    Can look you in the eye and read a number.
    And if you tremble they can tell you why:
    You are the knowledge that will drag its feet
    Like a disease unless we watch your step.

    Unless you keep stride with the street that we
    Parade together in the needle's eye,
    Shadows will smear your body like a swamp
    And link your feet before the unfed hounds
    That bay all divagations of the heart.

II Obscure in flesh, a dancer's earliest thought,
The crime begins, an instep greened with fern
Pathless as water, a feeling alone and first,
As with no motive, as a naked foot
Descends to the judgment of the copperhead.

Like venom to the struck heart, before you hear,
You feel your motive, in the mouths of hounds.
The unthinkable extreme's but a step away;
More terrible than flak vomiting opal,
The green of fern like morphine winds your bones.

Turn back, for though you stand brimful of blood
The frantic pack hunting you, tight wineskin,
Will turn, if you turn from this cul-de-sac.
It opens on silence, toward the word of men.
But if you run you will limp like a god.

Quick as a spark flowing out of flame
The great cat leaps along the snowy ledge;
It has no need, like yours, when the hounds bell
Bravura up the esplanade of snow,
To sled a snarling black doubt at its throat.

III   Deep is our grief. But no one grieves. We expire,
Easily blameless, in a padded chair;
The paper crackles in the Sunday sunlight,
The whole mind lifts and quickens on that wick
As if we had no other way to burn.

Yet I concede pride's pool, that mirrorful,
Aflare with the armadas of a day:
Science like elate Longfellow's Ship of State,
Praises about the prow, factory-loud
Midships scattering light, a peacock wake;

The arts, bucentaur on a seething calm,
Like beetles inching; coracles of God
Swashed in the wash of church and synagogue;
Barges and battles, pleasure and pomp and state,
Beside the keel of steel that speeds the race.

This too is burning. I've admired that brazier
Bright as a pond in the proprietary
Eye of a child who is lord of a stone
That could burst all: kick of a waterspout,
Over his toys it topples in his hands.

IV   And you, who heard the hounds instantly far
Hush, have not moved, through moonlight to moondown
Have heard no colder dark than an owl's question
Not meant for you, no dusk but the poorwill.
Why do you tremble to feel, at your throat, dawn?

Remember that rasped cry and whistling mew
That made a bony thought grow on the ground
And men of horror in a morning sun
Stand stripped to gristle. All shook like hounds. Like men
All curled their hands on satin gunbarrels.

But one, among them all, catlike looked down,
Only in their dream fellowed on his bough,
Torn tearer and avenger. The dissolute heart,
Muddling blood, living its old nature,
Monstrously confuses fury: man-dog-panther.

Beyond that blood, in blood what wild way leads?
Perfectly pathless: so the saints conceived
A lion's discipline. Braver, more free than
The foot of evil must be the feet of love,
That walk only on the water of light.

II

THE CATCH

The track of a broad rattler, dragged over dust at dawn, led us
Across the flats of morning under mesquite and paloverdes,
Path direct as hunger, up to a heaped grace of shade
Rodents had riddled into a hill of galleries. There it ended.

We dug into dust to take alive a lord of venom, whole
Rope and writhe as thick as a child's thigh, in halls of his Hell.

But what we found, under a crust crumpling to knives of spades,
Was a path of fury: earth as light and loose as a harrow beds,
Smell of plowland cut and clawed, and darker down in the mound
A sprawling rag of dragon's pearly armor slubbered with mud.

The feasting grave trembled. It shook us. We heard the darkness
           grunt.
A snout full of snarls, of a hound or a hog, heaved the spade up
           and dug under.

But was stopped in its tunneling by the steel, as steel was stopped
           in its teeth. It turned
Quick, clawing and snapping up light, it charged and a choker
           rolled it at pole's end
A badger strap-throttled, flipping like a marlin, battling like a
           bull on a gaff
And snoring anger till over his bravery and scuffling the door of a
           cage clapped.

Burrowing bearclaws rattled in tin. He tasted wire all round.
He bucked, he bruised the ceiling, lunged at a beam and was
                eating oakwood.

But for that ravening he lived unfed and unslaked. His stench was
                immense,
His dung was the curved needle ribs of reptiles.   He never slept —
Daylong, nightlong. His furious freedom resounded. At starlit dawn
Jaws and claws rasping and thudding thump of his thunder
                drummed once. Long

Silences rang for him, cage-eater greedy of snakes, abroad
                in the dawn.

THE NET BREAKER

I laid down my long net in the big tide.
The brown web streamed like a dropped sail in the water
Yet seemed small as lace. It lifted and rode,
Widened and lagged. Then it began to flash,
Shivering, gleamed, and sank with a long shudder.
I never knew what hurried and held it hard.
The weight of a million? Or one vaster shape?
The slack of it rose, floating the Niles of calm,
Idling over the rolling of the deepened ocean.

ORCA

21

Beastblack under a fin torpedo-swift
In a glaze of sun offshore that is torn with motion
Whales like gods of the dolphins flip and fall
And pour the lift of their dives like the surf's backs.

Slant of their fins asway like a wing speeding
And heads rising blunt like a feeding swallow's
They circle, black and white in their green foam,
With ease of swallows over the water, in air.

What they are feeding on we believe we know.

These are the steep rocks, white with guano
Over the deep seethe and list of the ocean,
That always re-echo the bark and bawl of sea lions.
A long while after the sheet of the sea is smooth
Only the gulls and the cormorants over their shadows
Will cross the light. And the brown rocks will cry.

KILLER WHALE, INSHORE

Cold from the glimmer of the undersea —
A bay of stone and green, greens, climbing green —
I strode with abalone in my hand,
Knees weakened by an hourlong sea, and saw
Near the bright shudder of my hunted reef
Orca, in that deep swirl I tasted still.

And I stepped like a child on attic stairs
When the whole house is built of silence: I
Stopped. Listening, child and man: The sea.
Often I'd longed to fling him from the world,
Knowing him far foraging, fearing him near,
My glitter lame beneath his sky-wide eye
While he rode ocean like a waterspout
Trailing a besom shade and trampled land
A peachblow-plucking cloud older than Easter.

Out of a calm he came straight as a wave
Bull heavy and dolphin sure the measured whale
With pied side sliding and hook a share in the air
Over the darkness trodden by his kind.
The green film at my feet climbed, calmed, and climbed.
He sank into the long unfaltering motion.

CARACARA

PAX VOBISCUM

Miles of that desert are the billion-flowering mallow,
Banner of orange broader than many vast horizons,
Paradisal light laid far under the thorns.
Out of the heart of light a caracara drops.
Tall along the dust among the buzzards hunched
Under the big cloaks of their flight's collapse, he steps
Shrugging yet circumspect, inspector of a feast
Bloating, skewered with legs, black ox on its back.

Before that servile watch that will not broach its meat
He moves as if alone, the one invited guest,
Erect, crested and pied, aristocratic, cold
Buzzard in hawk's clothing, nodding his badge of red,
Bowing his beak to touch — in the blast of wings
Disheveling to tread the feast — his wineskin on the dust.

Vultures may have been here once. But the bones
Unwrapped by the wet roadside, bogged in rainwater,
Are no longer choice. Only this dog
Like a feeding mummy tears at a tar of flesh
And shivers in the black pool poisoned with its food.

This is survival — not death, of a cur, cherished in his village,
Not far from a city, on the highway between the wars.

MARLIN

The wand of that fisherman witching the waves
Dips,
Feeling an abyss,
Lifts
Shuddering, buckling. It has hooked the tide.

Heartstring out of his reel
Screams, the sea
Fountains pieces of itself vomiting its vitals
Far from the boat
Something falling leaping

Skips like a keel —
Is up!
Brandishing, brandishing, a muscle, a rib: an arm,
Like God's
Torn off alive.

Tireless, until — as if the tide itself
Failed or the sea
Changed,
No more averse
Gave up its secret with strange irony

Under shrill-screaming unseemly seabirds' crisscross
Of augury —
Slow as a floating lily, mottled with sea-glyphs, fingered by the waters
Like an island,
Like its own sundown it glides in to die.

FOR THE *BESTIARY*

Our inordinate morning
comes

like a creature only a dream can believe in, drops
like a tiger down
from a cliff,

loose and light as a tossed rug; but suddenly
the ledge he alights at
stubs

a bulk of sinew stopped; he falls like a painted
bull's-hide, edge
down.

Come, he will not eat a man — or a child:
he'll rush among us
like a bad

moment before the coffee steams in the cup.
He has eaten: a Lamb,
a Dove.

III

SEA

I This handful of ocean water clearer than glass
Is like the mind at morning when it lies
Still in the palm of sleep, before it feels
Its forces shoreward combing the green eelgrass,
Fuming sand from the seaground, marshalling a myriad
Glimmering fishlights to mote the glory of the sun.
Even under the cornices of the Poles
The ocean, lidded with twilight, dreams monsters:
Hot whales, and the cold creatures that are mostly water —
But all are issue of the dust. The clear
Water here in my hand is full of dust,
Dissolvings of life and death: powder of fire
And sea-born earth returned to the using sea.
And used, will banner the tide with long algae
And thousand every drop with diatoms,
Will star and urchin, will lion the bald rock.

The sea lion sleeks its face in the kind sea.
I too, the shoreling man, have not forgotten.
Scatterings of skull with the shards and shattered shells
Of the headland lie with their kind. Out of the sea
That fed it, the domed abalone colored with calm
Of westward morning on the ocean; out of the sea

36

The skull that was gilled in its mother's belly; out of
The sea of sea-born mind the shell-like shard
Rippled on the rim by man's benthonic thumb.
And once far inland in a humming room
I saw my love undressed to the bone before me
And, in its lattice cage, that undersea
Creature her living heart dancing its tide.

I will go down to the ocean when I am dead,
Will ocean my ash, marry my dust to the water
That thought of us. For I see that we are the ocean
Walking the land with feet of the dust. We are use:
As much as the sea worm coiled like a stone snake
In the tidal pool, crested like ancient Mars,
A clouding of the crystal of the sea.

II   And I have not forgotten how a shark rolls
Feeding, while the kind sea sluices his smile,
Nor killer whale's brief breath, hot pluff of fog
Stinking of flesh. With eyes brine-blurred I have seen
A bag of jellied death in the undersway.
And I have smelled carrion on the high hills.

Our lofty wars hiding in height drone over
Their farrow rootling into flesh of cities.
Instruments of more aspiring mind
Point into orbit, fettled for our thought
Whose smoky flaw pushes them where we will.

Slowly the buzzards circle to decision;
Heavying, they drop, bouncing like injured airplanes
Beside the heap the hot sun cooks for them
And the maggots dolphining in the dust.

III When armies walk, sometimes in the dry of the earth
Their wheels smoke dissolution like a banner
Before them flown or after or candled high,
The flaunt of all their trackless history,
Their powdery past, their secret yet-to-be.
And like that banner slacked along the waves
Is the mortal stain rolling upon a coast
Of rainy storm. Mix of the cloudy land
With roil of nameless slime and chyme of weed
And sea worms' houses crushed, riffles and churns.
In that chaos the pride of death is downed
Like a streamer that has floated awhile.
And any swimmer in the finishing chop
Will feel his joints smoother with fear, may feel
His courage warm his throat like frosty mint
While dark under his breast the glidings suck.
For there, below him, the filled ditch of sleep.
Therein no coming gleams. What treasures pearl
The bottom of the waves? His dream shall fathom.
But in the dawn his soul swims back to him,
With hands like fins and seadepth eyes staring
And lips that drink the brine. Perhaps it swam
In circles in the deep. Perhaps it found
The floor-end precipice, and looked . . . and looked.

IV   From that old landend that keeps Dana's name
     But not the shape he found in his century,
     Pale sift simooms in summer; in the winter rains,
     Conglomerate comes down and an earth stain —
     And sometimes flowers. All round it the busy sea.
     No silence trembles in those bouldered halls
     We dare in calm but the sea's silken fret.
     We hear the crumbling of a century,
     Or an eternity. But when we shake
     The fires and shadows from our eyes and climb
     Over the cliffs, we find some things that came
     Out of these crumblings: sage, and pointed grass,
     And changing flowers. There sometimes the octopus-eyed
     Rattlesnake glides in the leisure of his venom,
     His scales whispering; a beetle prints
     His stipple in the dust. And a clawed creature
     Standing with dangling hands stares at the south
     Rolling the midday waste of riding fires.

I have walked in a vineyard by the cliff
And break of the long land over the long
Monotonies: there eating the ripe grapes
I have held remembrance in my ears:
When I lay down for sleep by the gray shade
Under the vines, my face against the dry,
I heard a sound like bees. Till my love came
Walking against the light, and shaded me.
This was that afternoon when first I traced
Her lineage to the foam, while her hair flowed
Like summer wind over her throat and mine.
We wished never to die. By the grape's blood,
The too-lush tendril clipped, the aphid crushed,
The steady vanishing of the water's flash;
By shapes and vanishings: shapes, vanishings . . . .
We heard salt rushings on the prow of land.
Lying as if in sleep, perhaps we slept.
And heard planes, drummings shaking the floor of sleep.

V Dust is rising in the earth — windwaked
It walks on the hills or in tall columns on
The talus plains hurled up a stairless height
Hangs . . . trackless. Over the sea torn leaves of lost
Letters of embassy bleached of their use
Blow down, atomic ghosts, fine increment
Into those sucking wells where all is drawn.
I have seen the fieriest moment of a life
Fading, gold smear in tidal mind, sea-shine
In the sludge of night, along the edge of sleep.

How many cry, If it were really so!
If these were not sea fruits with tight juices
The air will dry to a difference. O if we too
Were not the thing we are, then we might be
Like idols that need not fear the rainy jungle,
Stilled in some sweet unequaled attitude
Timelong like stones.
      So we inherit those
Brown nomads of the rusty-colored earth
Who heaped hard walls, their new Jerusalem,
Precious shelter, out of the way of time.

VI It is long since first the sea sent up beyond
Its margin ambassadors to the courts of death,
To the stand and stillness germinal unrest
In shells of form, creatures of earth but also
Of the waves' vagaries. Breathers of change,
How did they learn to love the unflowing rock
And found their houses there? Why do they choose
The heresy of stone? Even where they hide
They hear the cry wiser than hope mounding in,
And run to pray in their dry citadels
Against their breath, their blood, and the ways of their dances.

The body of the brown world is beautiful —
Idol out of the blue vague of the sea.
Prairies are under the oiled hooves of riders,
Morning breezes trample the scent of grain
To the red hills with the passes blue among them,
And clouds beyond are watching the unknown earth
Their shadows stain. And no wall of an ending,
Only the halt in the dusk by the poppy fires

And dawns of discovery under a setting star.
What is my life before me? How shall I say
Except that I feel the horizons under my breastbone?
We race all day in the open world till evening
And when the embers click and the acid crickets
Are loudening we lean to our sleep. And at last descend
The valley of home, trample the heels of memory,
The ash we scattered to the morning star.
The dry sound of our hands shifts on the walls
At morning as we stroke the doorframe thought.

Beautiful to us therefore the winds' violence,
The lifted modulations of the dust,
The dry hills that are called everlasting
Vague in the veils of their mortality.

VII In bowls of a foamless ebb I saw the water
Rolling the home of one of its old aspects;
The skull clicked on the rocks, emptier than when

44

Loaded with jellies it played business or love.
And plucked from the wash, sluiced of its drink, it seemed
Too draughty a home even for the butterfly
That flitted from it to the Elysian fields.

I dropped it back, to cradle in the rocky shallow.

Once universe poured through it freely as there
The sea-gush slid or while it lay too slight
In hand the loose wind. Dead or alive,
Brimming ambiguous music like a shell —
What is it but a husk of whispers. Breathless,
It sighed to me: "I grieve to think how I wasted,
When I was dressed in delight, my dearth of hours
In being so careful to shun both pain and filth.
I would be glad, having the brown dung
Daubing my flesh or blood flowing from it —
Now I am a clicking system of reminders."
I answer it: Be silent. Your voice, too,
Is the sigh of a dream, irrelevance of my heart
Because I have turned away my ears from the sea.
The grieving is all my own, the cry of regret
Is mine, because I am detained by dreams:
This one, of afterdeath, and all those thousands.

VIII Up the clogged shallows of a long inlet
Lagooned in ooze that slows the sweetening tide,
Who dreams the tidal wave, a tiger sea,
And fears the swirl of doubt around his knees?
Has he not seen dead time in heaps of shell
On any strand, or from a broken rock
The fluted stones emerge into the sun
And sure abrasive of the winds' feathering?
Beneath his terror housed on crumbling piers
I hear the music of the ceaseless shore.
And the out-tide and the in-tide of his heart.

Who dreams of Truth, of immortality,
Of forms to live forever? Nor shall he lie
Uncounted in the exchequers of dust.

Let him be comforted: let him unbind
The ringing dreams from his scared ears and he
Shall listen to the water at its work,
Washings of sleep under him, shorespeech, sloshings
Garbling his little errors till he can hear
All blend, smooth to the diapason Sea.

IX   What is the sea, the gray cartographer
Who always loved her single blue can tell:
The universal pool, a stoup of sleep,
That rounds the letter of our care with smooth.
And he who rivered all his freshet days
To irremediable salt believes he knows.
The child too, dabbling in the instant wave.
And the anemone, beaten with foam?
What is the sea, lensed to a moray brain
Whose life is hunger, whose reach is tipped with teeth?
(As ours is delicately thorned with thought.)
And to the swimmer daring the sunward blaze
Beneath unbuttressed light, the unvaulted nave,
Taking into his mouth the salt and fire
Of noon enormous as the nestling's autumn?

I will not believe only the desperate midden,
Though all its references are to the sea
I cannot disbelieve. I will not dig
In the black heap to find tomorrow, narrow
As the long flint, the bird with folded wings
That hissed in flight, the testimonial fang,
That dolphins there. I will believe the sea.
It horned the desert hills with ammonites

Before there were hands in Egypt or the moon
Shone upon Ashtoreth. Persisting whisper,
It breathes in all conspiracies of dust.
It breathed the wave that wrote, as for a sign
On the white sand, the light whorls of her hair.

X I can foretell no form: before us lie
Horizons empty as the heart's expectation
On the shore of morning, the sea's clear promises
Until the end. If end. Our language questions
Mainly itself, a tangled theorem spread
Straining in the elemental tide
To take those glittering shoals that swarm and pass.

And all these names are lies: the gannet's bath,
The Pacific, the Dark, the User. That sea is not
What we believe, but something past belief;
That tone we love most is its cry of escape
Out of our categories as it names
Forever a new name for namers' ears:
Never itself. O word, where is thy sting?

XI I stood alone, hearing the sea drain down
Like memory around the established rocks
And flood enormous present up the shore,
I heard the antiphonal death and birth of waves
Covering silence like membranes lying over
Immanifest undoubted life. I thought
Of music heard in the night: beneath my head
The heart of one I love, the ways of the sea,
Epithalamion and threnody,
The changes of the water and the dust,
And silence under every syllable.

THE WHEEL

Rolled out of surf that wheeled upon itself
And burst but left a whirling in a head,
Up light and land the given danger crushed
Toward harvest home or a short scream. And still
The unfallen image rocking like Juggernaut
Tamps the tangent of the axledance.
The wheel has had its way. Multiplied millions
Gride in the ruts, circle, or simply sit
Quivering and singing: Wheels without end, Amen.
Rattle of a penny in a punched machine:
Dropping onto wealth in privy darkness, bronze
Piles up. Wheels within wheels within belief
Upon belief heave the bright gears that fold
Like praying fingers grind like cursing teeth
And unclasp like the laughter in an ad
And close, and pinch the stamping die, once more
The just cliché, and press the whirl that hurls
The onward face.
                      Ask and it shall be given:
Underneath are the everlasting wheels.

II The air has filled with vapor white as milk
On the azure ocean: gunfire brought by the wind.
Southward into the sun our fear continues
Aloud: tramplers assembled under San Clemente
Along the horizon are proving our usual courses.
Think, while the windows are rattling in their sockets, what power
Is trying the strength of the house by day. A thief
And an angel. For shall not that tread tremble again,
Hoof of the chariot of Phaëthon that yesterday we plunged
Into Hiroshima, thudding its fountain cloud?

The winds winnow dung for the merry sparrows.
The long clouds go over and look down
On desolations as they have done before.
What are the chosen species? And for how long?
We too have enjoyed the services of the elements
And from the grounds of our enjoyment have argued
The tolerance of a loving God.
Now the moult of that wing launches more snow.
Ulcers and other fears, even the words
Of the most wild among us, deny our wisdom —
To whom we begin to listen — saboteurs
Whose hammering doubt rings on the old gages
Unsound notes, a throb to be stopped by the wide
Palm of authority raised, the arm clublike.
For life must go on. Death must go on. (Therefore.)

III   No shore so soiled but speaks in the sea's tongue
A little: glaucous and glairy wash, wavering
At morning beside the city cliffs of La Jolla,
Toward noon the gull-loud bathers' urinous tub —
Yet foam by the seawall rides as under a prow.

Better the unwatched tossings (except by the birds
Facing the winds' music on the scoured shelves)
Borderward. There, few swimmers. For even in calm
The guttural black hides bathe, hairy monsters
Coned with the rose of slicing barnacles,
And do not care. Even into pretty crystal
Where nothing drowns, swallowers with leathery fans
Of balance in the long stroke of seaground sliding
Broach the subject of evil like a dream.

Blunt stumps color that water. Yes, on my tongue
There is blood, a word we have not endured. Blood in
My heart, blood black under my ear in the night.

And here we are almost finished smoothing away
The rough and ready work of our warmen's hands.
Surgeons are out of work, looking for work,
And we send them home for a rest. For our arms are pointing
The way to final peace. The statesmen roar
To the statesmen: Lie down like a lamb! Nations covered
With live wires of trajectories kneel in foxholes

Praying like racers.... get ready.... The dark of my theme
Gathers on the street corners — names no day....
The repetitions of the wheel ascend
All high places, fill up with honey light
At evening the target towers.

IV Up from the sea, Palinurus, like an insect:
But for those fine, thin plastic struts in the corslet
Planes might envy, he is all soft within,
The bone of the body outward for defense,
Russet and bloodbrown plated, flanged and horned.
Guarded by thorn, his tender sight aswivel
Bulges in beads of plexiglass on stems;
Touch wands about him like a pair of whips.
Hooks on the hinged tail are claw and tooth.

Ocean made him out of the equal dust:
Curious; beautiful, even — not seen in a mirror.
We would rather be strange after our own fashion.
Would rather be not strange: with tooth and claw

Will cling to all we seem — to claw and tooth,
To the names of our fathers, to their named ways.

There was a man that woke in his father's house
From the son's sleep, a roach. In the son's bed.
Even he who has never given himself to any
Darkness but sleep guarded by the patient clock
Will know I have spoken of the terror of death.

V   Who will submit himself to change shall endure
Uncertainties wider than the blank ocean
Under no star, his raft the iron wheel,
His oar the axle: a grain for grinding, a straw
Broken for the division of the waves.

But how should we require this of ourselves?

Easy — burning curled autumn or the winter
Husk of April. But to reap down wantonly
Unfallen things for the rakes' paws and the sweet

Tooth of insatiable fire . . . to roll
Security away — a pretty penny —
Seaward silvering, swelling huger than fortune
Till far in the foam it turns like a bedding dog . . . .

Let it be given, like dust, to the ocean.
Then it may climb wavelike into the light,
If ever again, with bloody felloes clean.
Or let it steep in the elemental crystal
With the most ancient stuff, the most washed, lost.

VI   Burnt offering, above it a blue calm
As over the cigarette of one who muses.
It was my sweet Belief. But now I see
It is the dust of return: the mirrors' smile,
The word, the finished house, the wheel that crushed.

Against the high autumn, combed cotton toys
Of the winds' miles, far airmen flash and drop
Like skiers watched, voiceless, swift on the slant
Of the avalanche. Azure without echo
Draws on our "End?" X etched on skidding ice,
A black cross, exact signature of will
Across that light, sweals into acid blue.

VII   You billions of pied mice fancied by chance,
          Performers of one dance
  In pretty printsteps round a maypole moving
  (No bloodier dancers ran the mazes of Crete),
       What if the maypoles of your trance
  Were not the only postulable poles . . .

  What if no axle stand among the stars?

          Children of ocean:
      Where little lemmings drown,
        Dances the dolphin
  That came from the water and returned,
       Homeless forever
    Among those wandering hills
That are built and broken swiftly as by living breath.

APHRODITE OF THE RETURN

Wading a waveless water, who is she
Who leans over our shadow, arm of darkness
Winding inland? I beside her there
Lifting the porcelain dish of Semele,
Rosed pearl, cup the discredited stream, gaze fireward
Toward evening's white delay, downslough, downworld
Where the breakwater snouts and a bell dangs
Like an insect crawling over the heart.
She is my love Anadyomene
Who rode the water tiles, the thrown roses
Around her and, beyond, the still sea and
Recessions of hunched coast, eternal walls.

The ferns are all unwound; the heavy spider
Is gone from the net. There now a few leaves spin.
Gathered by the gray squirrel in the brittle bracken,
The golden bulbs of laurel, fruit of strange sweetness —
I would not calm the spouting sands nor freeze
The speed of the sun, chain up a chainless dance.
Turn, year, that brought her feet into my bed.

She is that one I housed from weathering
In the museum of my love.

II Old Dragon, Father: tidal crocodile . . . .
What other children? Daughters and sons of Dagon,
Or the dressed horde, none of them beautiful
Enough.
              The bawl of the sea bulges like thunder.

What if no dawn should bring us to the sand
But with obsequious bowing, forehead down
And blue lips kissing like the loveless fish?
I think of him who sees over the waves'
Broad evening where he swims, a smoke of stars
Rise like a sacrifice he cannot name
And turns his face to the inexhaustible
Under that image of necessity.
Let her turn round and wade the shifting foam,
Aphrodite of the return, beneath
Her curving feet the chill of ocean moving,
Aphrodite clothed in the threadless air.

Shall we be lost from your ways in a rage of waters?
The waves are under your houses shaking the pillared
Postulates. And I have remembered dolphins
Stitching the sea, sheltering only in their act,
As a running needle clothes itself in the garment.

IV

PROGRESS REPORT

Skipjack sun in his long leap
   ocean to ocean
   describes our hope.

The requisite mettle, a new kind of thought,
   is picking the lock
   that holds the heart.

We wait only to earn a way
   not to be lost,
   to vault on the fatal

light till the earth has gone like a drop
   from a thorn in the dark,
   then to revolve

the night and, not to the stars' or the moons'
   targets, fall
   home to the pool.

ON A MONUMENT
ORANGE EMPIRE TROLLEY MUSEUM

Hulks of the end of the line,
Cold wreckage, hot with paint,
Idols of iron and glass
Poise afloat in a bright
Sargasso paradise.

Whipped to our hopes on a million
Gleaming parallels,
We saw the infinite:
Pinched by their tips of steel,
The point and end of speed.

Faithful, on that sea-reach,
We leaned from city to city,
Between the island green
Vineyards and groves of sweet,
Till there was no more sea.

CORTE MADERA HILL

When the train rattles on its iron
Far off on green marshes,
I remember how it is flung
Between humped hills to a tunnel
And under, humming dizzily
In the highest of those hills.

How long a mile of electric
Quiet is swaying amid black,
In neither life nor death,
Flowing as before birth
When there was no help,
For now is all, forever.

That highest of those hills
Is topped with rock and laurel,
Windblocked laurel and rock;
But it has a black look
For all who remember in it
An enduring instant.

Through the eternal tunnel
The old spell, unhope,
Holds. Then with an ashen
Flurry white day flashes:
Earth and the sky — light
Like a million doves flying.

Far across the marshes,
Raising a heron's harsh
Terror out of a pool,
Under heights of laurel
And low pasture hills,
Unending cries diminish.

UPLAND

SUM OF SUMMER

This is the winds' country. Stillness here
Is the held breath of pines, aspens' tapping,
Tissues of silence after sounds of grass.
The hot crackle of grasshoppers cannot end it,
The rattle of autumn rain, the ticking sleet.
But leaves' hissings, whatever breath the pines
Resume, far off the wind chafing its flumes . . . .

Here in the hard hills, wind is freedom:
South to stir us, and the nightbreath, and all to undo
The absolute with processions of dust, snow-smoke,
Vapor combing over iron blades,
Island ingots at evening opening the west.

Here is the eagle's climb, unwinking wings
Rising and silver loss and the standing sky;
The blunt word of the wind at our lonely ears;
The wild grass white with the wind's body.

Where the green steamed in ribbons shoulder high,
I saw the topaz in the bittern's eye.

AUGURY

The loud
Dove that came out of China
Forty years past and was few,
But now is dove of houses and groves,
Is courting, calling,
Fluttering as if he rose on a chimney of heat
Over the green canyon against the wedge and flat of sea
To his height, his drop in a glide away to the tip of the tree
That came here over the ocean also,
But early, out of the south:
He drops to the long boughs lolling in wind,
To his mate on a naked crook
In shimmer and click of falcate leaves.
He nods, and puffs his roseate breast like a valentine,
Raucous cock of the light he has taken, the hour, the morning despoiled
Of the mood that watches still the cliffs of the farthest island
Traced in air of the water of the west,
As it was before we changers came to this coast:
The brush crouched to the wind, the wren-tit's terraces,
Cliff-edge seeding space with silt
Over sea-freed boulders,
The upland distance rising and rounding away
Through silence,
Muted coo
Of the mourning dove.

TRACT

HIS BABYLONIAN HEART

That long
Chore of bulldozers
Chewing those hills above us into amazing
And pitiful preconceptions,
Making our world into real estate
(Id est, unreal),
Is over.

The hawk,
The owl are gone.
Weasel and fox and deer, that nobody saw,
Were gone as the clank began
On the land that rose so stony and steep.
It had no value
At all.

Under the brown cliff that gives over into fire,
Into afternoon's angerless undoing, all
The humps and horns of its brows and the butterfly-
Brilliant crumble of its scaly hide,

Under the landfall, on the sand by the unfailing
Tidework and teething glitter, a child is raising
In the felling light ancestral towers. Far
Sunward, Babel's zikkurat tumbles in the waves.

NOCTURNE: LAGUNA BEACH

Suburbia crowns her hill between inland smog and changing ocean:
Long houses crenelate steeps too tilted for building,
Wind's-browse and raven-rock, still to be mastered.

At twilight when the first streetlamps lift their still constellations,
Hour when coyotes shaped their music
Running the dusk's rabbit
Under the tumbled steeps of wild Aliso,

Lights of the little cages along the canyon crest
Yap at each other
As if they were hearing, beyond the waste of decades, something
Invisible, like the first color of stars in the void over a city.

The red larkspur stands in dust under asphalt.
The prairie wolves are dead.
The dark ages are ending.
The cities are solving their problems.
The country is at peace.

LIGHT

When the poles have gone under the gauzes of our fog and a withering of icecaps
Is watering our deserts and dikes are rising and land is too little
Despite the high piers fattening into cities and beyond them suburban
Archipelagos of barges broadening our pleasure on all of the earth's
Waters and the moon our quarry is blazing from pockets of her rock
And powdering from her cut mountains and uplifting from the smelters of her plains
The breath of our life and over her light is curling and curving
The opal of glaucoma our night will long have been blinded of far
More than her brilliance that will have preceded the sun and have followed
Out of heaven the stars we were reading a little as they tarried into exile.

VANTAGE

All over the blue
Ocean the trees of the whales' breath:
All over the ocean,
Around the steeps of the headland
Falling westward and northward,
Punta Banda, and southward toward the turn of the land,
        three hundred miles,
Toward the lagoons, the pools of calm on the coast of deserts:
The fountains of the breath of the beasts
Whitening and leaning in the wind
On the ocean curve of the world,
Floating and misting,
Into mist
        into distance
                into light.

The time is not yet
Of the continent-cities
And the forests cut.

When our age of glass is no more
Than glitter in dunes

Of detritus
The clouds will be here
In season, the water
Always.

The regret will be gone.

II Ocean and air will lift
Shoring combers pluming
Over their leaning green
In landwind wings of spume.

If creatures astir on the cliffs
Have then the gift of light, let it
Be larger than ours, that lost
The world and took the moon.

V

IN SEARCH OF MAN

Some labyrinths curl round like a sea shell;
Even in Crete, that was the ancient form
That Ariadne's wreath led Theseus down
Before her brilliance ravelled to a thread.
As far and deep, in such a sounding place,
Like a black pool or the Minoan hole,
Dark as the Minotaur I have walked with him,
Careless of that faint wraith my landling image
That heard our tread like flukes and loved the sea.

What is a man? Not only one of those
Images. I listen for water, voices on voices
As of the multitudinous truth of inmost
Sentience, other breath than any language,
Music that, if it visited our tongues,
Would underhum like a voice amid surds.
This is, perhaps, a sound that is something like
The impossible definition of a man.

But who of all that listen can hear the sea?
Ranging the gamut of a billion shores
But falling, for the immemorial ear,
Only on one, it is heard after a fashion.
It speaks, like a pebble, of old times

And of the ancient principle of attrition
Liquid and plosive in immediate shingle.
It has nothing to say about the deep
Unless by saying nothing, or all but nothing,
In full measures of ease that like a heart's rest
Gather the energies of the overbeat
Out of complexity.
                    Though Theseus lived,
Though all the ransomed seven and seven came
To the sun and the dancing floor untorn by horn,
I look askance — into a cenotaph:
None saw the body of dead Minotaur.
I too have killed fears in a labyrinth:
Brindled morays, fishes with necks like bulls'
Under a wave, shadows. But not that shadow
The black sail of returning Theseus mourned —
For one had died; in the doubtful labyrinth
An image died. It had a form the god
Ocean in ancient ages had, the bull
Neck, the bull head.
                         What is a man, Theseus?
Aegeus the king your father believed the sail
Darkening toward him over the Aegean.
However that blow came, the abrupt brunt

Shouldered him from the rock: he grieved and died.
You mourned, in purple. Called by a later shame —
Ariadne's sister Phaedra, your wife, roped high
Like a mute bell swaying for Hippolytus —
A bull out of the sea punished your pride.
Again you heard shores crying ai! ai! as when
You left the sister of the bull for bride,
On stony Naxos, to the ambiguous god.

LEARNING THE LANGUAGE

The diphthongs are honey, the dentals are resin
Between the teeth: and, tasting, I can see:
This country comes into my standing car
Like the scent of orange blossoms,
Like dust blown from the plow,
Like the woman who asks — and enters, as the barrier rises
From the crossing and naked rails while one
Slate-dark train flows from the station
Away toward emptier plains, more pallid
Distance piled with mountains of haze.
Under the lintel of cloth over her brow the eyes,
That were keeping their counsel, black as a cave whose own
      darkness is its door, change:
In the blank of their shadow, a brazier is breathed on.

ANSWERING A LETTER FROM A YOUNGER POET

What shall I say but, having written for use,
I am glad, hearing that others shape, with words
Made for my ear and stride, a life like mine.
To await the recommendation of death
Is to tell oneself secrets, like the mad.

Gregarious man, the loneliest animal,
Varying even from himself always,
May envy the conclusion of the dove
The brutal seasons charm, daylong aloft
In his high cool defined and redefined:
The invariable being of a bird.

I think of the young, who must think much of war,
Little of being. But will find in wars
A unison (their anguish) nearly love's.

II Lawrence and Bishop were the men I chose,
Because they made of momentary ways
Their being. All their light walked over water
And sought a man commensurate with light
And found him multiple as the glassy ghost
Of Proteus we wrestle in the sea.

How shall we endure change? Swimmers who deal
With shadows subtler than the octopus,
Who brave what nicors died in Beowulf's boast
And dare the shoaling combers' cold turbines
Yet tire of the open, ride inshorings, wade,
Look to the land where happier beings close
Hand upon hand or blade to know themselves,
Far from the garden of the waves' whitening rose.

Meditating changes in a stone
I think of dust, that scared stone-worshippers;
Of water, where even dust is dimmed or lost;
Of dark, gathering that turbulence.
And know why Bishop painted a green dawn
And praised its wind, how in the salt of touch
Those men divined a measure, then a thought.

III Twenty-five years ago alone in foam
Between the brown and blue of noon I climbed
The hill of change in instantaneous flame
Up the thrown slope of an enormous wave
To a height toppling like a bathing swan.

A wave like Paradise. On the small sand
Love in a stillness watched the wide ocean.
Poised between love and death, I seemed to choose
The shore. But I chose both: fury of change,
Earth and ocean, furies of a man.

I have found no definition of a man
But in that change, where now you hear and move.
Even in that loneliest wave we are not alone.

ASCENT

I swam the high moment of the foam
And the foam fell, freedom of light,
Graces of innumerable dissolutions
Between the grave and the shark.

The land could not tell me what to do.
Only the slanting cold, assembling vast
Changes and interchanges, the body and light
Of a sequence older than death, collected my heart.

Immemorial ocean aflow and alight in a high
Comber lifted a process of white succession
Arising like ages of angels floating and fanning
And folding plumes over the fallen sand.

In the scud of the trough, I breathed the ever
Unfallen crest of the moment forever forming:
Everest air, over the hillock years
Fainting like wakes of waves in the waters' light.

TEACHING MY SONS
TO DIVE FOR ABALONE

We waded pools, the piling
    Ebb, pull
Of a wild of light, and swam,
    Irons in our hands
And foam colder than iron.

    Over the deep
Of the ridges slow as a sigh,
    We breathed, we dipped
To the west, lurched to the stone
    Light of the land.

Seal-like we rode in a green
    Lunge or drawn
Deep in a dusk of foam
    Fishlike, quick
Of the tide, shifted together,

    Swung and rose
As if the hiding moon
    Looked all her light
On the play of wild things free
    Of the whole of her foam.

MOMENT BY MOMENT

Your hair on my breath
In leather of fallen
   Leaves,
You gaze into light,
   You see
The wind overhead
Whetting the crescent
   Green.
Bare as a rope,
   Our hill
All round us opens
   And falls:
   Silence
Covers our path.
Under my hand,
   Breathe

And unclasp your hands,
Loosen the past
   Away.
Up from the hill's
   Apron
The oval west,
   The sea,
   Is breathing.
   High
In the sweet of the vast
Fig of the morning
   Flames
Our mortal sun.

LOVE LETTER

Passing and passing
in my grey house
you are always putting to shame
the splendor of the angels.

Don't think of this. . . . Listen:
the ordinary sparrows.

I found it between
a thought and a thought.

Something is growing,
changing alive
under the fallen
leaves of words.

RETURN TO THE NIGHT

On rote
Of rubber we rode
Over asphalt horizons
Under the white
Fir and the blue
Spruce,

Down
the tight curves
To slack and spread
Of land, lake,
The late meadows,
September

Afternoon
Cooling its shadows.
That water rippling
Reeds on its sky,
That house we found,
Sufficed:

A room,
Scent of wood
Warming the doorway
(Already dusk
In corners), a table,
A bed.

Walking
The shortening plank
Of a pier we came
To the end of haste —
And mouth to mouth
Of peace.

Late,
By the window, wine
Darkened. We stepped
In the wind's tracks.
Like moths we danced
And learned.

Night,
The powdery thick
Of the stars from the zenith
Down undiminished
Around us, lawless
Shone.

FOR LOVE: A SHIFT

105

I have wanted a thing like nothing:
Your body bright in fame of a cloth so subtle it would make
The eyes of envy close
And open only into praise.

One way to change the world.

*

I have seen the world change like a scowl,
The tradesmen smile.

*

The look of paths when we were young was the look of the path.

We stayed in the moment forever:
We changed
In the endless instant.

*

"Tomorrow it will be ready."

The body clothed in tomorrow
Is ragged and patched with hopes.

But tomorrow!
Tomorrow, the wearers of tomorrow
Will dress a la mode:
Wrapped into cloth so fine the weft and warp are one.

*

We easily turned from the path,
To the dusk of the bench and the poorwills,
Having no time to gain
Or lose, being paid by the moment.
Then we had nothing to buy.
We could afford to go naked,

One way of changing the world.

VI

The poems in Part VI, written in Italian and published in an Italian journal, are related in theme to those preceding them. Thinking some readers might want English versions, yet unsatisfied that any preserved the life of the poems, I have made merely literal translations, deviating only in the slightest ways to keep some integrity of rhythm and ensure precision of meaning.
                                    B.G.

HOMAGE   OMAGGIO

In that language — Italian, I am on the high seas.
The phrase, lips and heart, thrusts onward
far and afar; the verse
like the comber over the reef
lives running, moment of light:
the wave is the waves, the tide
throughout all of the ocean.

PORT   PORTO

Birds on the waters far out, gleams
of feathers, gray and unquiet
like the first snowfalls
of autumn.

And now
all is simplified
for our eyes: expression
of the terrible complexity of the heart.

Nella lingua italiana sono al largo.
La frase, labbra e cuore, sospinge
lontano lontano; il verso
come maroso sopra lo scoglio
viva corrente, momento di luce:
l'onda è le onde, la marea
per tutto il mare.

Uccelli sulle acque di lontano, barlumi
di piume, grigi e inquieti
come le prime nevicate
d'autunno.

Ed ora
tutt'è semplificato
per gli occhi: espressione
della terribile complessità del cuore.

PRESENT   PRESENTE

They go talking, the swallows
over the orchards amid the rocks,
where the peach trees illumined
with earliest sparks

are changing the shadow of winter
toward noonday and summer,
the peach trees without voice, immotile
in the rose of the moment.

SOUTHWIND   AUSTRO

Unforeseen is my love:
it is born in the amplitude of the sea,
in the empty space of the temple open to the wind
that comes to the flowers of March, to the grass of September,
when on the wild hills
is sighing the flight of the world.

Like naked feet over invisible paths,
like the leonine mane of summer of a girl,
it comes and it passes.

Vanno parlando, le rondini
sopra gli orti fra le rocce,
dove i peschi accesi
delle prime scintille

cangiano l'ombra d'inverno
verso mezzogiorno ed estate,
i peschi senza voce, immoti
nella rosa dell'istante.

Impreveduto è il mio amore:
nasce nell'ampiezza del mare,
nello spazio vuoto del tempio aperto al vento
che viene ai fiori di Marzo, all'erba di Settembre,
quando sui colli deserti
sospira il volo del mondo.

Come i piedi nudi sui sentieri invisibili,
come la chioma leonina di una ragazza,
viene e passa.

ANNUNCIATION   ANNUNZIAZIONE

They are burning, the forms of the perpetual beginning of life,
gold noonday of spirit,
in the moment that changes and forever is the same fire.

It is far from us, far from the streets' mechanical rumble
and the lifted mad finger that signals terror and tears
in the penal dusk of the city,
and passes atremble,
and once more in the dark tree darkening on the sky between houses
sounds out forgotten spring,
the bird trilling unstilled.

I turn anew to the forms aswarm
in the infinite net of the light
at the heart of Florence,
to the wings outspread and upfolded,
to the glory over Gabriel and Mary,
seven angels surrounding the dove of God
like the swallows at their nests in the air of the walls.

Ardono le forme dell'inizio perpetuo della vita,
oro di meriggio dello spirito,
nel momento che cangia e per sempre è lo stesso fuoco.

E' lontano da noi, lontano dal rumore macchinale nelle vie
e dal dito levato impazzito che segnala paura e lacrime
nel crepuscolo penale della città,
e passa tremante,
e ancora nell'albero scuro e più scuro sul cielo tra le case
suona la dimenticata primavera,
l'uccello che trilla e non tace.

Torno di nuovo alle forme brulicanti
nella rete infinita della luce
al cuor di Firenze,
alle ali aperte e chiuse,
alla gloria sopra Gabriele e Maria,
sette angeli attorno la colomba di Dio
come le rondini ai nidi nell'aria delle mura.

MAN

    I inherit the salt
of the sea. But I do not know
what has happened
in my heart, oceanic
secret son
separated from the past
and from me.
                The waves leap,
ancient wheels broken one
by one falling. I have heard
in the sounds the vast blood
touching the unknown earth.

UOMO

Ricevo in eredità il sale
marino. Ma non so
che cosa è avvenuto
nel cuore oceanico
segreto figliuolo
separato dal passato
e da me.   Saltano le onde,
ruote rotte antiche a una
a una cadendo. Ho udito
nei rumori il sangue immenso
la terra ignota toccare.